This book belongs to:

....

In loving memory of:

....

Story text copyright © Tracey Bell 2011
Design copyright © Joanne Diffin 2011

The right of Tracey Bell to be identified as the author of this work has been asserted
by her in accordance with the Copyright, Designs and Patents Act 1988.
Image copyright Waterlily & 57847111 used under license from shutterstock.com 2011

BRIDGE CHRISTIAN LITERATURE

First published in 2011 by Bridge Christian Literature
Printed in Northern Ireland by Graphic Answers, Tandragee

ALL RIGHTS RESERVED

No part of this publication may be reproduced, stored in a retrieval
system, or transmitted, in any form or by any means, electronic, mechanical, photocopying,
recording or otherwise, without prior permission in writing of the author, Tracey Bell.

Scripture quotations taken from the Holy Bible, NEW INTERNATIONAL VERSION®.
Copyright © 1973, 1978, 1984 by Biblica, Inc. All rights reserved worldwide. Used by permission.

British Library Cataloguing in Publication Data
A record for this book is available from the British Library

ISBN: 978-0-9570491-0-9

www.facebook.com/loveneverends.co.uk

Love Never Ends

A book to help comfort children
suffering bereavement.

Tracey Bell

By Tracey Bell

To: Lee
Lots of Love
From: Mum & Dad
Happy Christmas 2011

Dedication:

I would like to dedicate "Love Never Ends" to the memory of my daddy, 'Big Harry' McClelland – worthy of everlasting love. I thank God that Daddy was a lovely part of my life, even though it was for such a short time.

This book, written from the heart, is based on the pain and heartache I felt after my Daddy died. Writing the book has been a difficult and emotional experience, and yet doing so has helped me deal with long hidden emotions, 22 years after daddy's death.

It is my prayer that this book will bless and help many children in their own journeys through bereavement. God brought me through and He can and will bring you through too – keep pressing on!

2 Corinthians 2: 3-4

"Praise be to the God and Father of our Lord Jesus Christ, the Father of compassion and the God of all comfort, who comforts us in all our troubles, so that we can comfort those in any trouble with the comfort we ourselves receive from God."

Acknowledgements:

I would like to express my sincere gratitude to the people without whom this book wouldn't have materialised.

Firstly, I would like to thank my very talented cousin Joanne for illustrating it and making the words come alive in a way I could never have imagined – I couldn't have done it without you.

To my printers, Graphic Answers, thank you for your patience, support, good humour and a job well done. I look forward to working with you more.

To those who sourced books to help me in my research and those who took time to read through my proofs - many thanks for your help and feedback.

I can't say thank you enough to all those individuals and groups who supported and publicised my fundraising efforts, for without you this book would still only be thoughts in my head. To all my wider family whose talents were put to good use throughout my fundraising – I owe you big-time! A special word of thanks goes to my lovely friend Aldrina for your encouragement from the outset and your investment and faith in me. Also, a big thank you goes to Steven and Andrea for your extra special fundraising efforts – I appreciate all the hard work that both of you put in – I'll never forget your kindness; and those blisters!

I would like to express my heartfelt thanks to my Mum for her emotional support and advice as well as her encouragement during both the highs and lows of my writing and fundraising - I know it hasn't been easy Mum.

Words are inadequate to thank my dear husband – you've been fantastic! Thank you for ignoring the fact that I broke the handbag rule (more than once). Thank you for your support and patience, especially during all those late nights at the computer, not forgetting an endless supply of tea and tissues!

Thanks are due to all those who have been faithful in their prayers for this book and me. Finally I want to thank my greatest encourager – my Heavenly Father, the complete expression of love; God who draws close to the broken hearted, who comforted me in my troubles, who collects all my tears in His bottle (Psalm 56:8) and who one day will wipe every tear from my eyes (Revelation 21:4). Nothing can separate me from His love. Love never ends (1 Corinthians 13:8).

Sarah had a little cat,
He was her closest friend.
Together they would have such fun,
and not want playtime to end.

On the grass they loved to play,
And chase the butterflies,
For hours and hours and
hours on end, beneath the
summer skies.

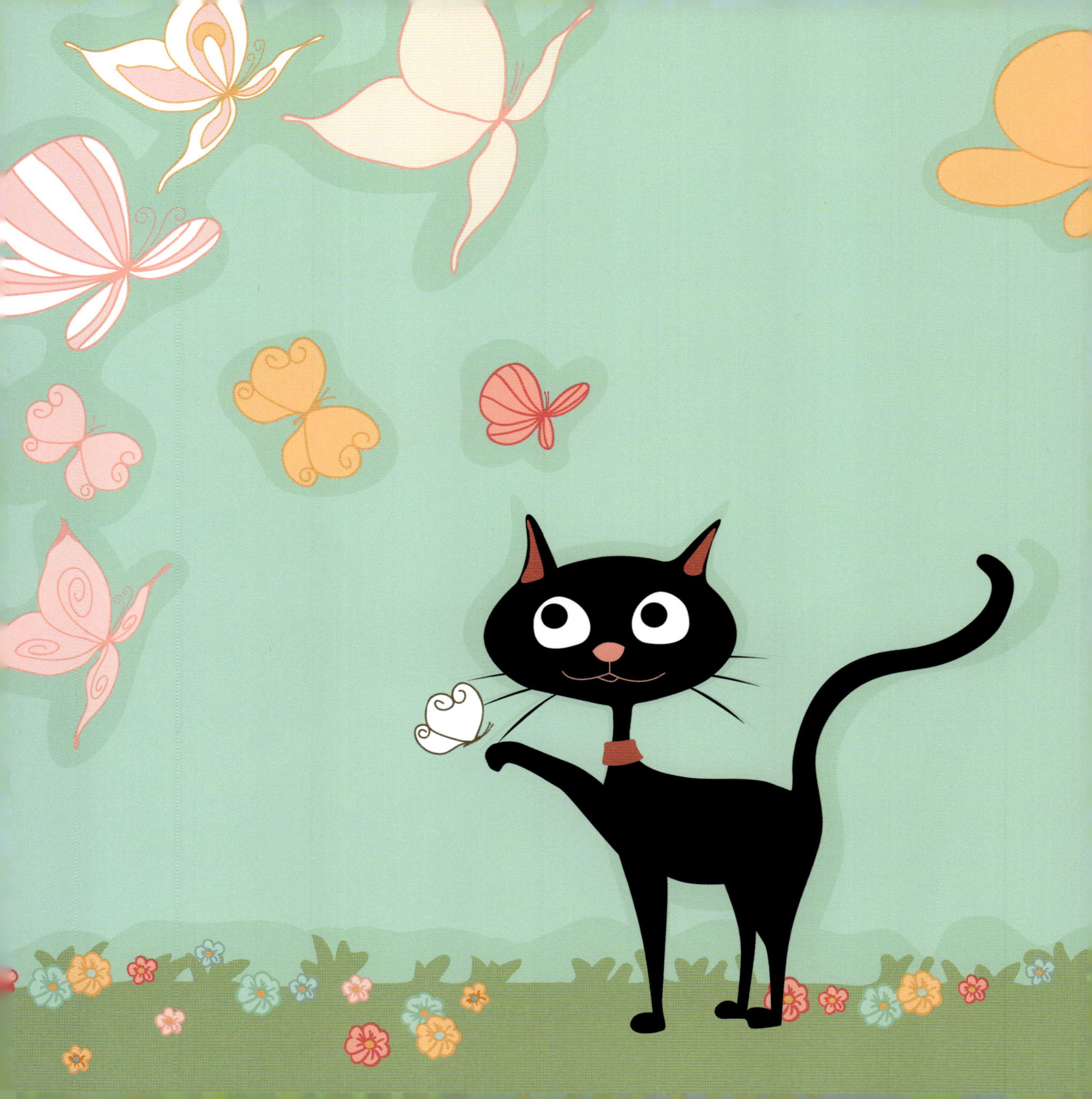

Sarah named him Shadow,
Because of his black fur,
And when she stroked him on the head,
He'd purr and purr and purr.

Sarah would make balls for him,
From out of bits of wool,
And he would run and hide them,
Beneath the kitchen stool.

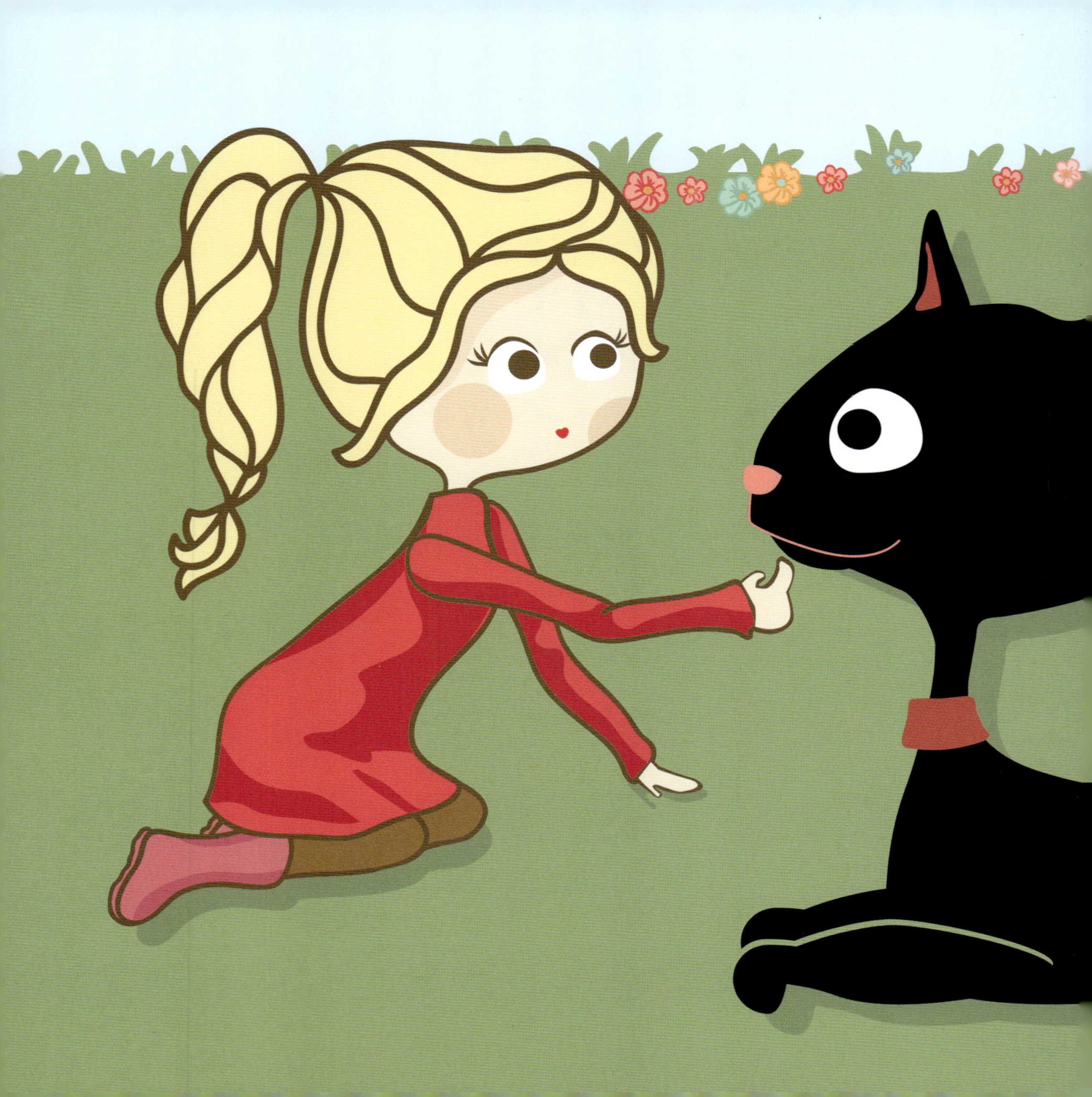

Shadow really loved the times,
When Sarah tickled him.
He'd climb on her and purr and purr,
For tickles on his chin.

But then one day when Sarah called,
And went to feed her cat,
He wasn't at his usual place,
Upon the back door mat.

Sarah called and called for him,
But Shadow did not come.
This worried child began to cry,
And ran to find her mum.

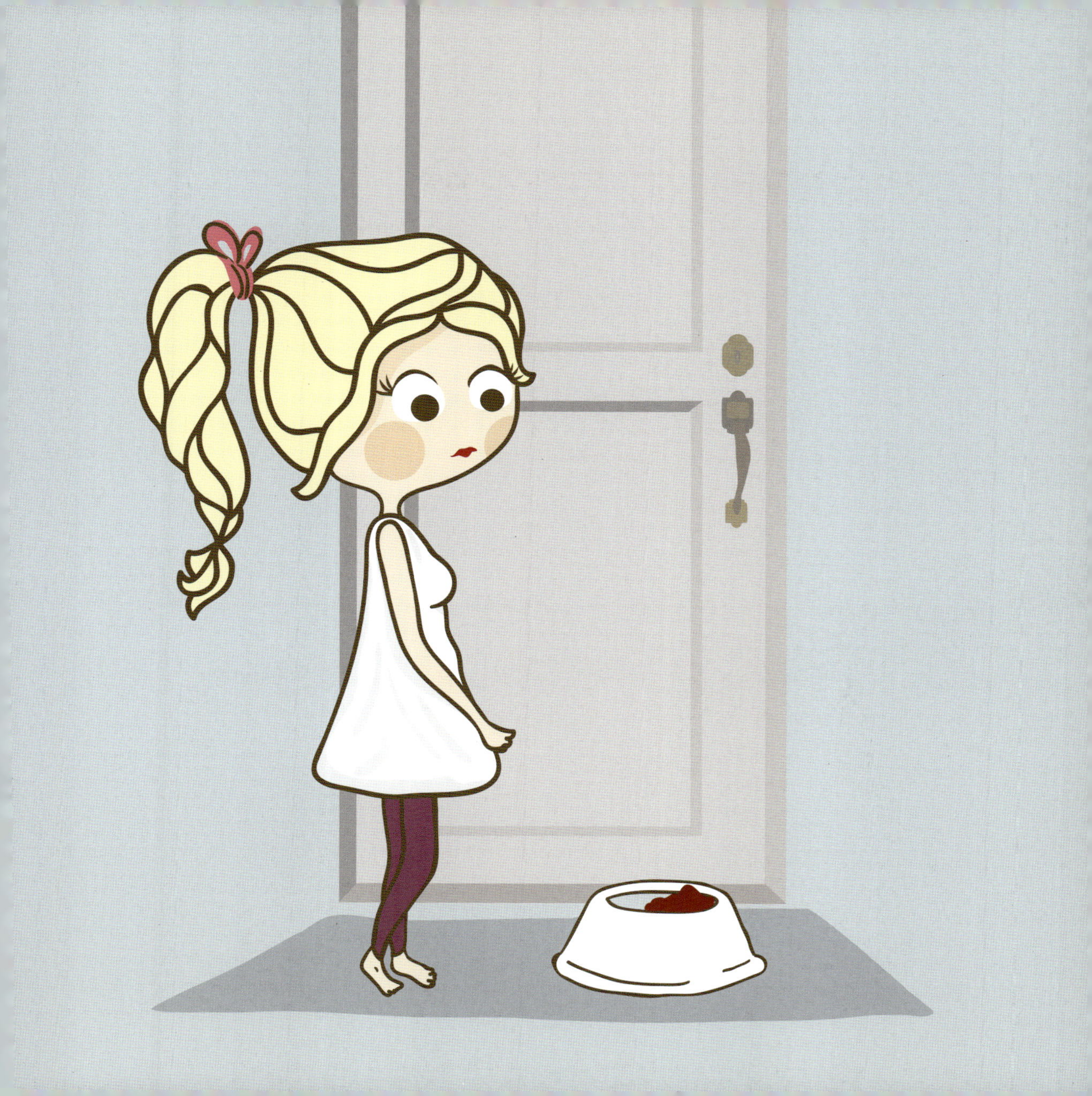

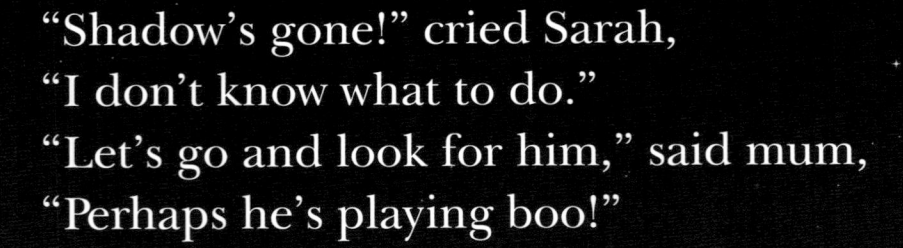

"Shadow's gone!" cried Sarah,
"I don't know what to do."
"Let's go and look for him," said mum,
"Perhaps he's playing boo!"

Mum and Sarah searched and searched,
And called and called and called.
They searched each tree,
Each neighbour's house,
Behind each garden wall.

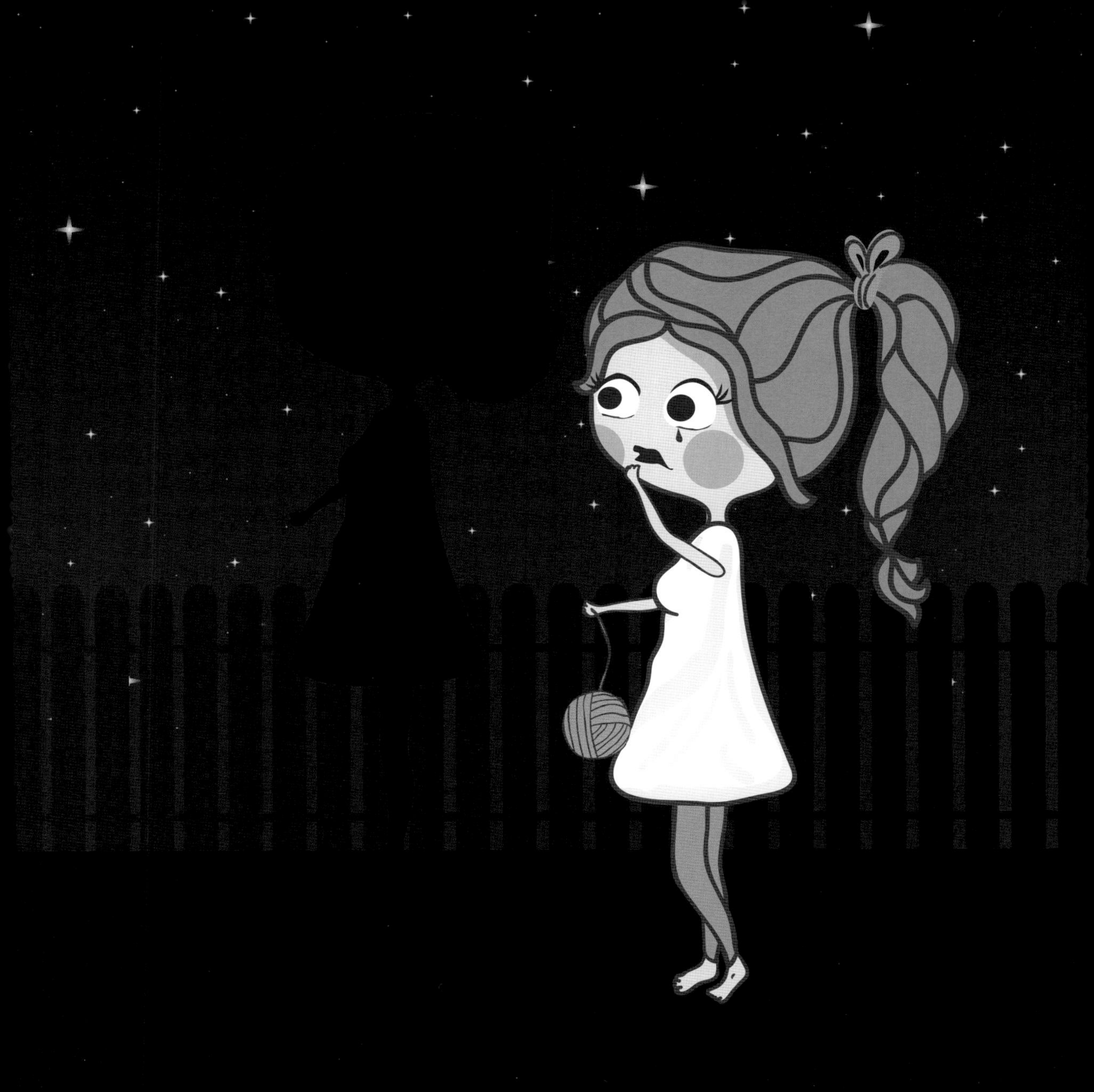

Then Sarah heard the doorbell ring,
Mum went to answer it.
The man next door was standing there,
He asked them both to sit.

He held a box with both his hands,
And tried hard to explain,
How Shadow had been in an accident,
That evening in the lane.

The driver hadn't seen him,
Until it was too late,
And now her little cat was dead.
Poor Sarah was a state.

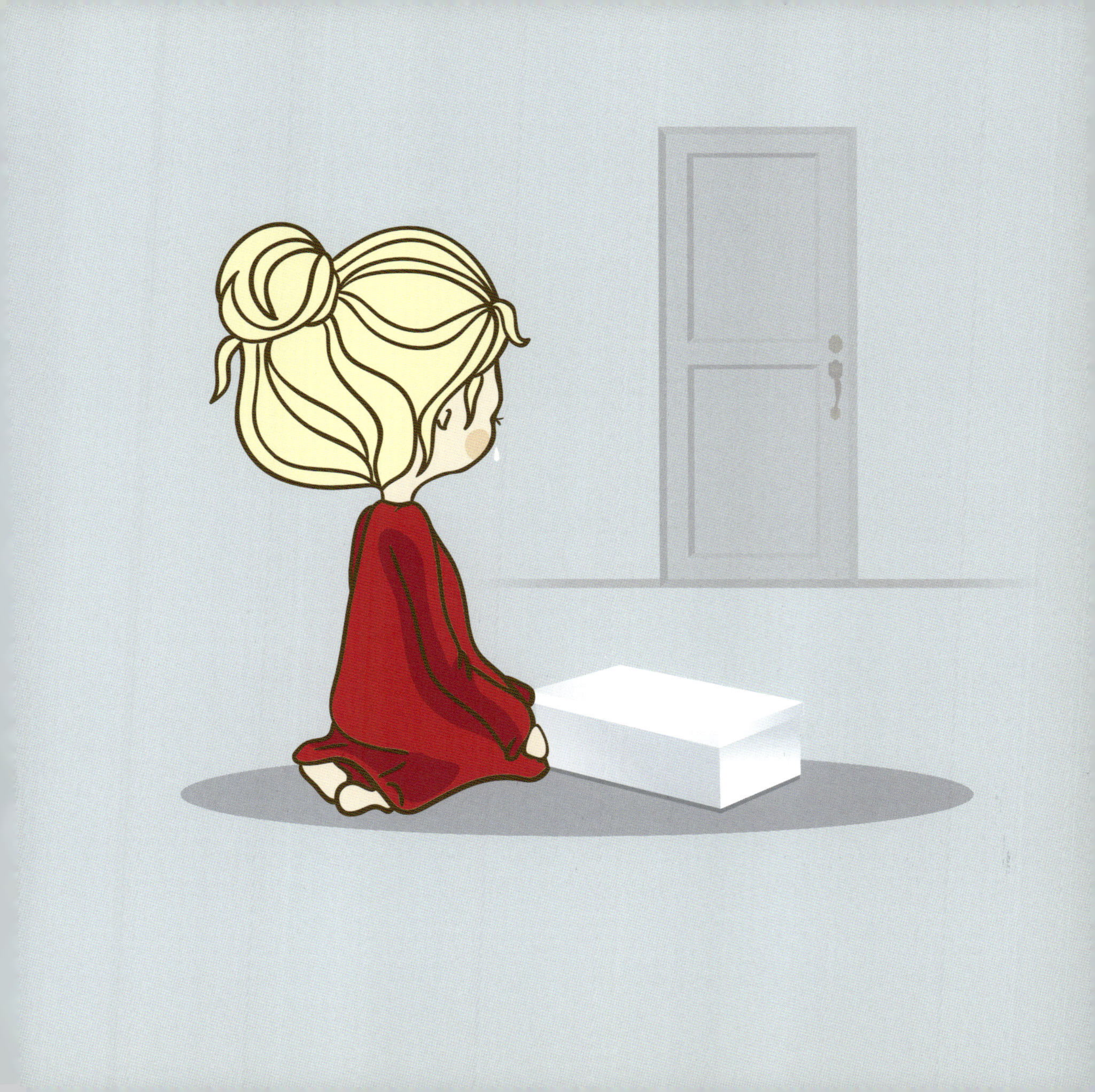

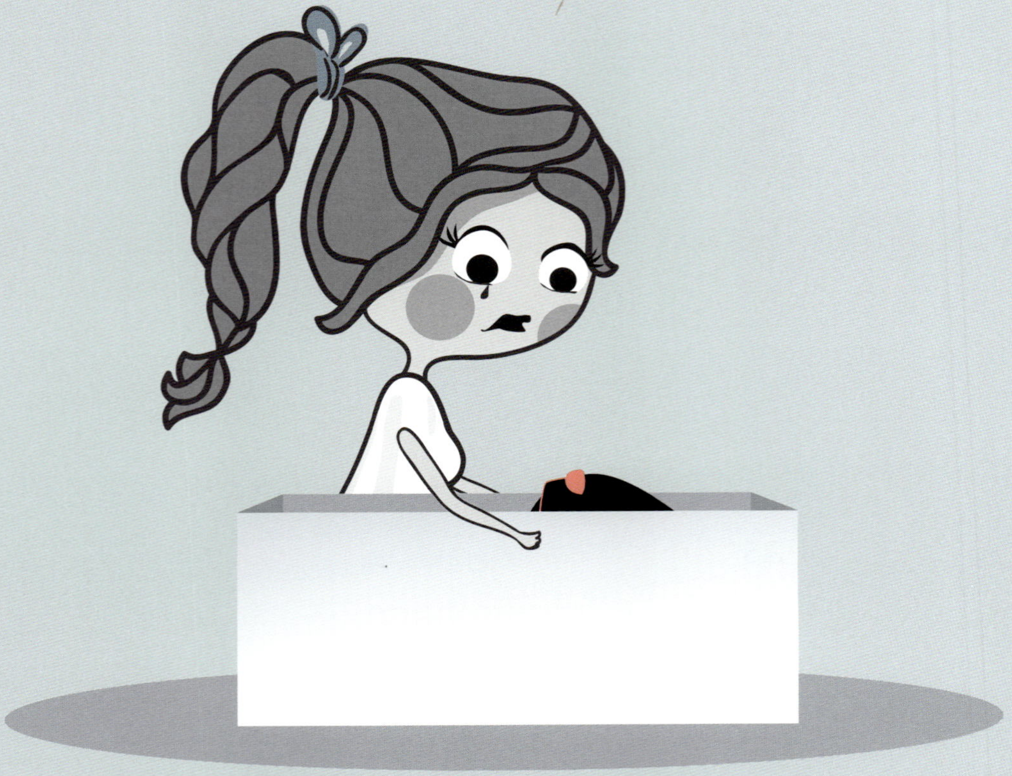

With trembling hands, she took the box.
His body lay inside.
She picked him up and held him close,
And cried and cried and cried.

He looked asleep just lying there.
Her hopes had turned to fears.
And as she stroked his soft black fur,
Her eyes were filled with tears.

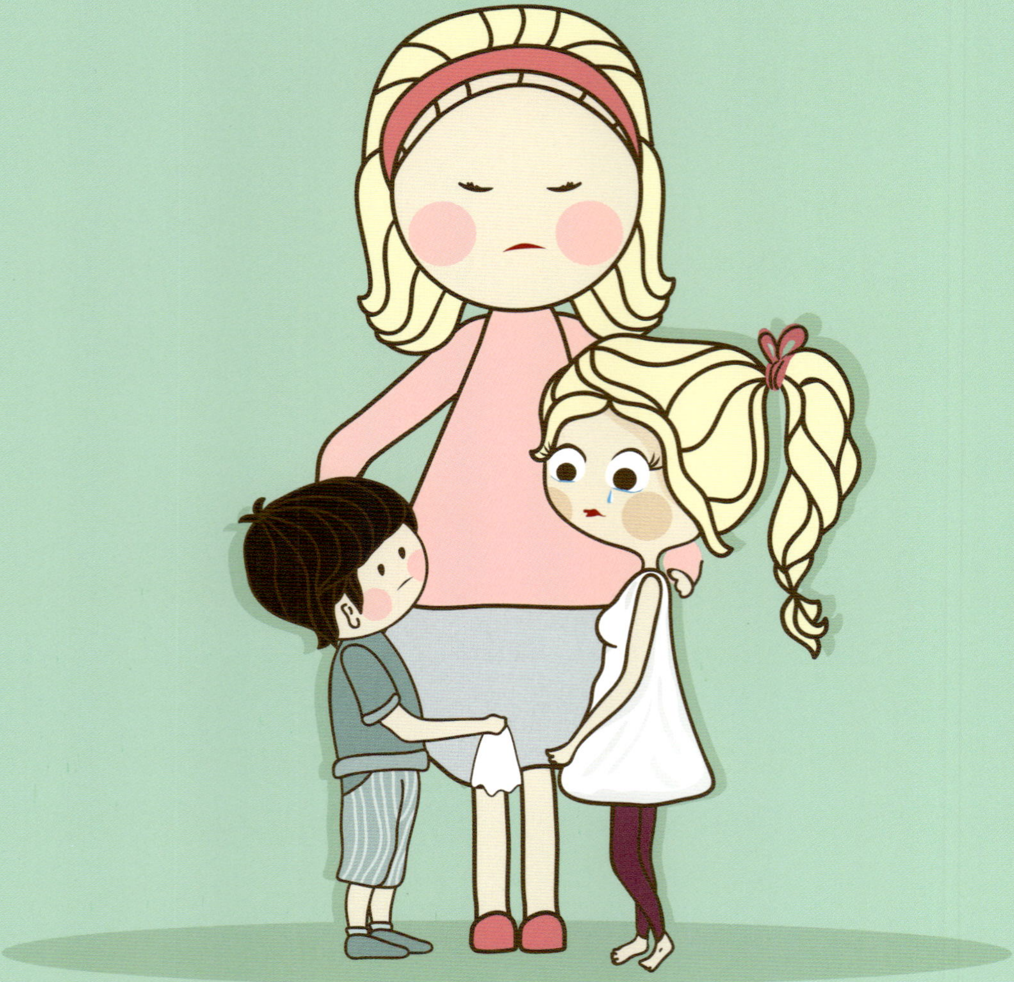

Mum took Sarah in her arms,
Brother Adam joined the hug.
"What happens now?" asked Adam,
And Sarah gave a shrug.

"Is Shadow ever coming back?"
Cried Sarah in a blur.
"If I cry tears into his eyes,
will he wake up and purr?"

Mum said, "I'm afraid not Sarah,
His life is at an end."
"I'll miss him mum!" cried Sarah,
"I'm alone without my friend."

Sarah's grief got worse and worse,
With every passing hour.
"It's all my fault," they heard her say,
"He got hit by that car."

"I should have looked after him better,
I should have loved him more.
It's all my fault our Shadow's dead,
And now my heart feels sore."

But when her mummy heard this,
She sat her on her knee,
"It's not your fault, don't say those things,
Just cuddle in to me."

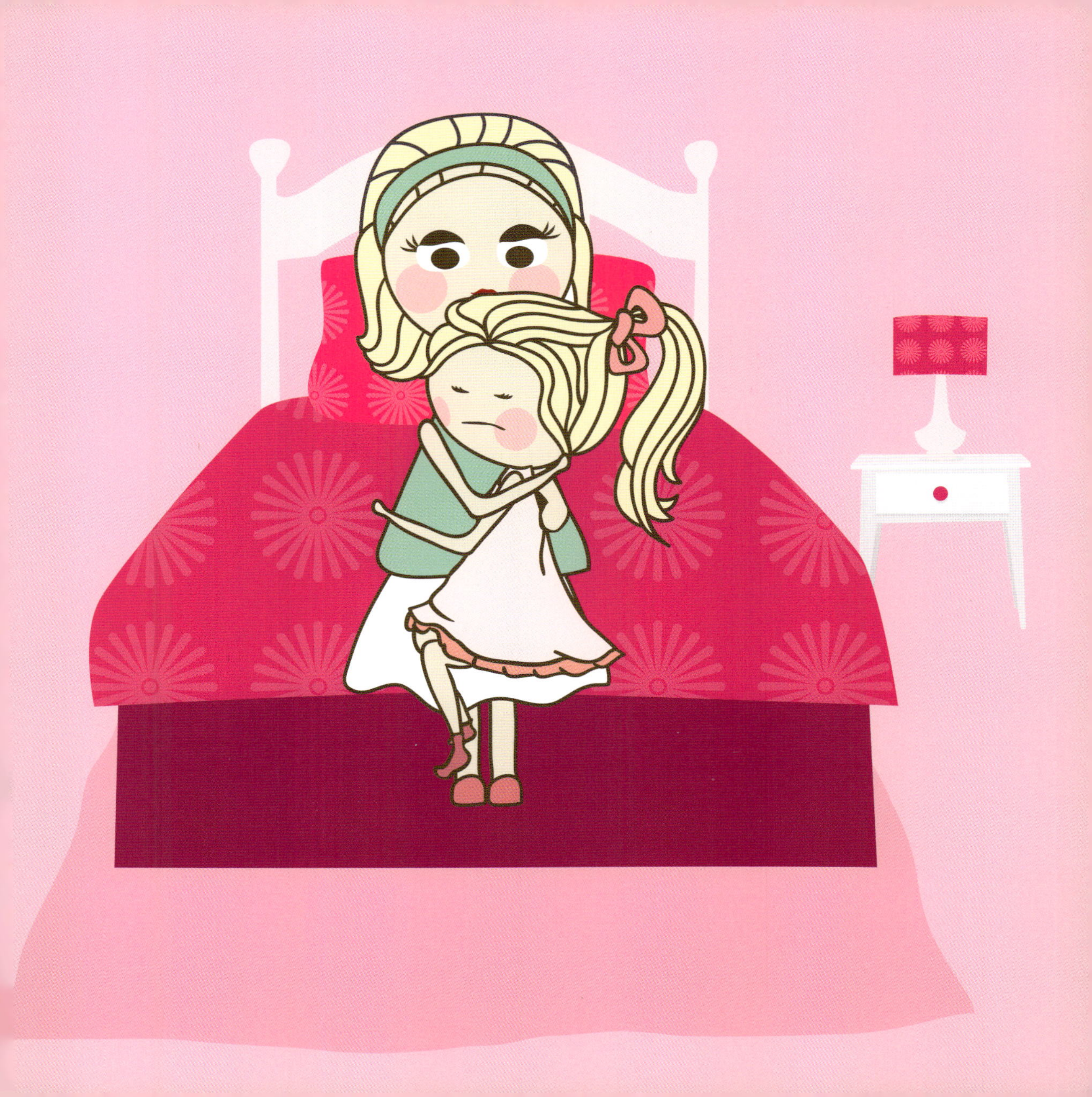

"Shadow knew you loved him,
So very, very much.
Love doesn't go away you know,
Just because you cannot touch."

They had a special service,
To remember their wee cat.
The box was buried in the ground,
Where Shadow often sat.

Mum said, "It's ok to feel angry,
To feel sad and to cry,
But think of all the happy times,
You had in days gone by."

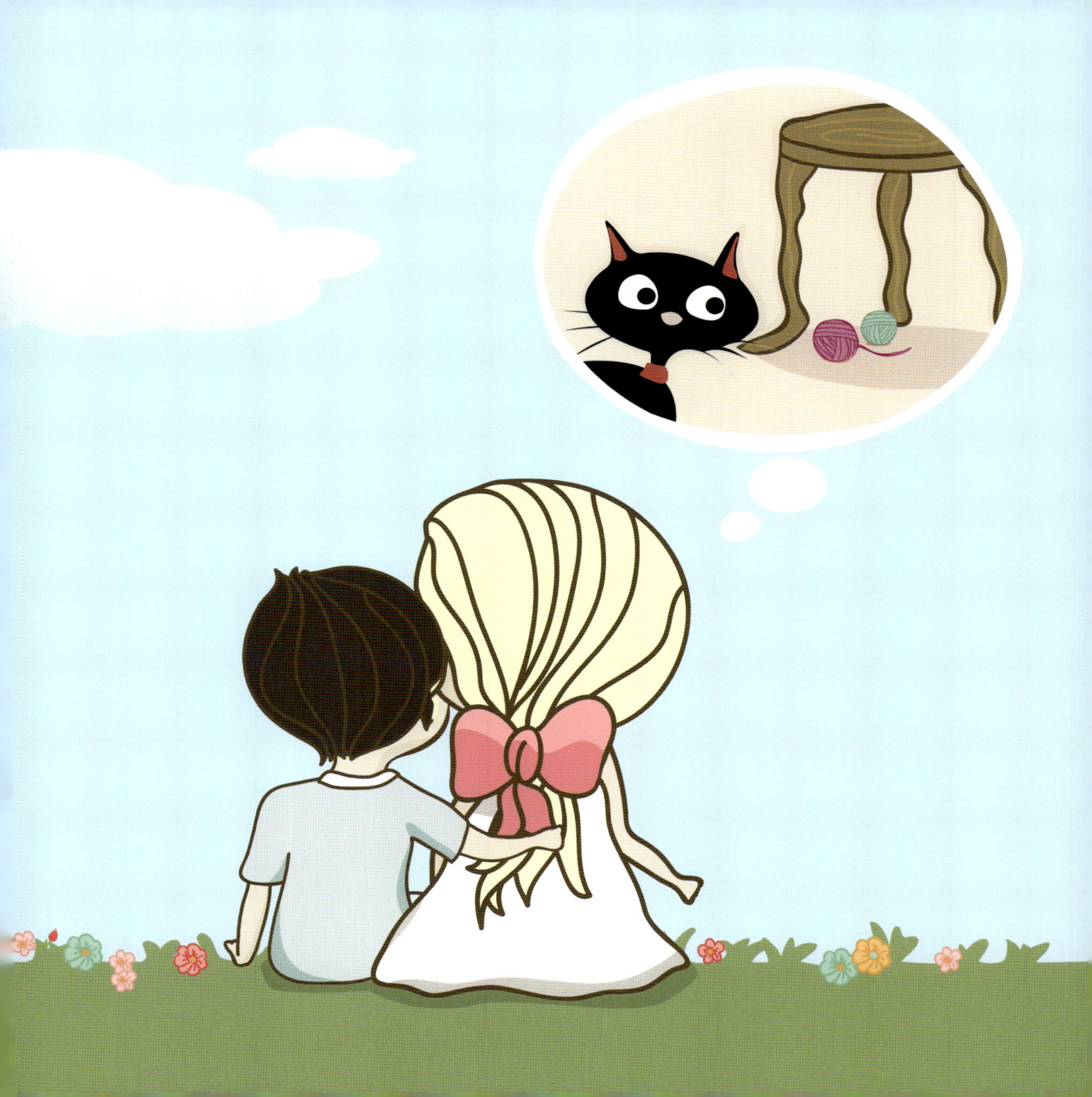

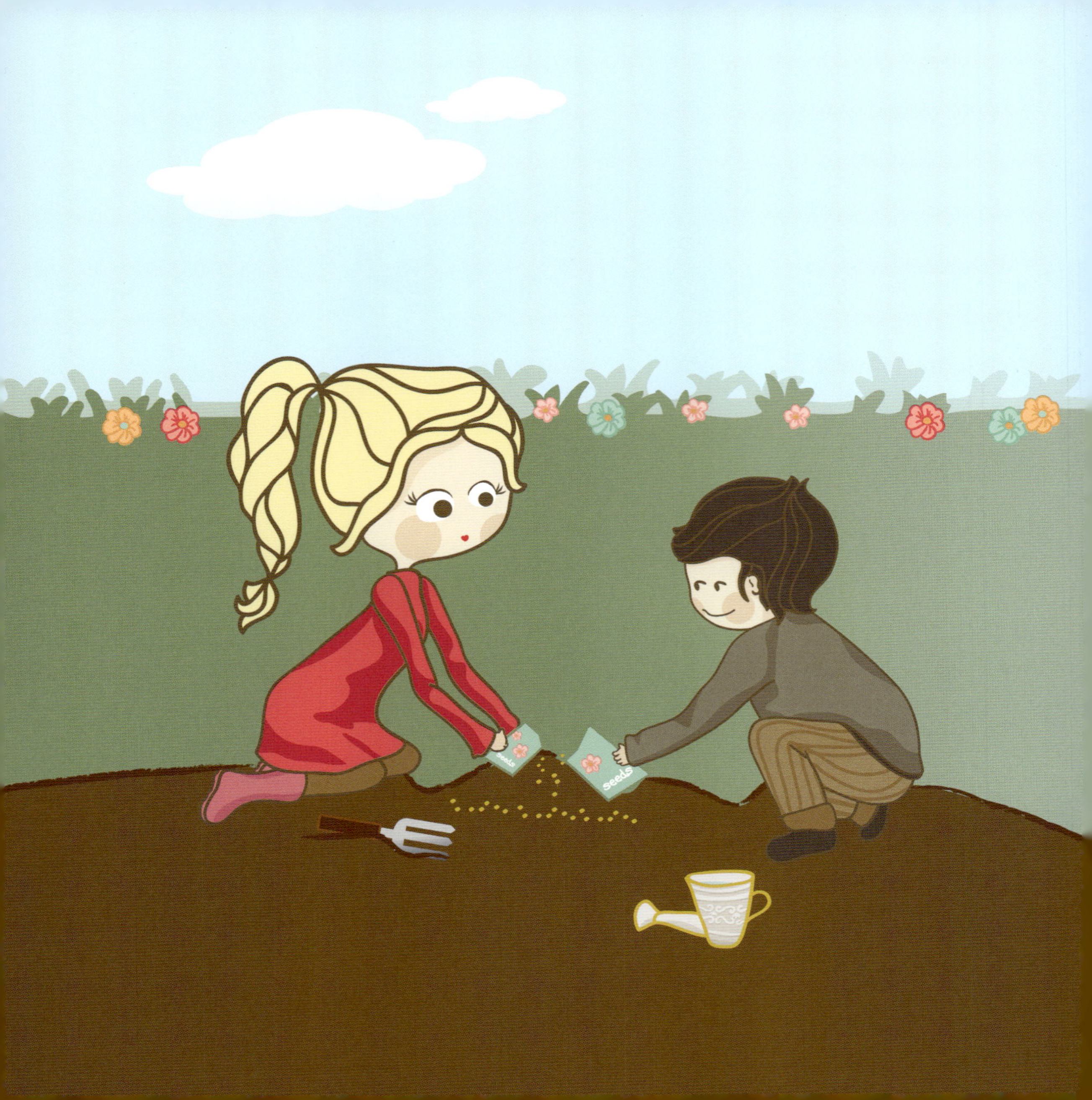
seeds
seeds

They planted seeds of a butterfly plant,
Where Shadow had been laid to rest,
So that when it attracted butterflies,
They'd remember him at his best.

Sarah felt a little better,
But still she'd often cry,
Because she wanted one more chance,
To kiss her cat goodbye.

Sarah still felt lonely,
Without her furry friend,
And she began to wonder,
Would this sadness never end.

"Grandad's in Heaven," said Sarah,
"Will Shadow be there too?"
"I'm not sure," her mummy said,
"But this I know is true,"

"Jesus has made a special place,
For all who love him dear.
He'll make heaven perfect for you,
And wipe away each tear."

Some things are very difficult,
To try to understand,
No matter what you feel inside,
God always holds your hand.

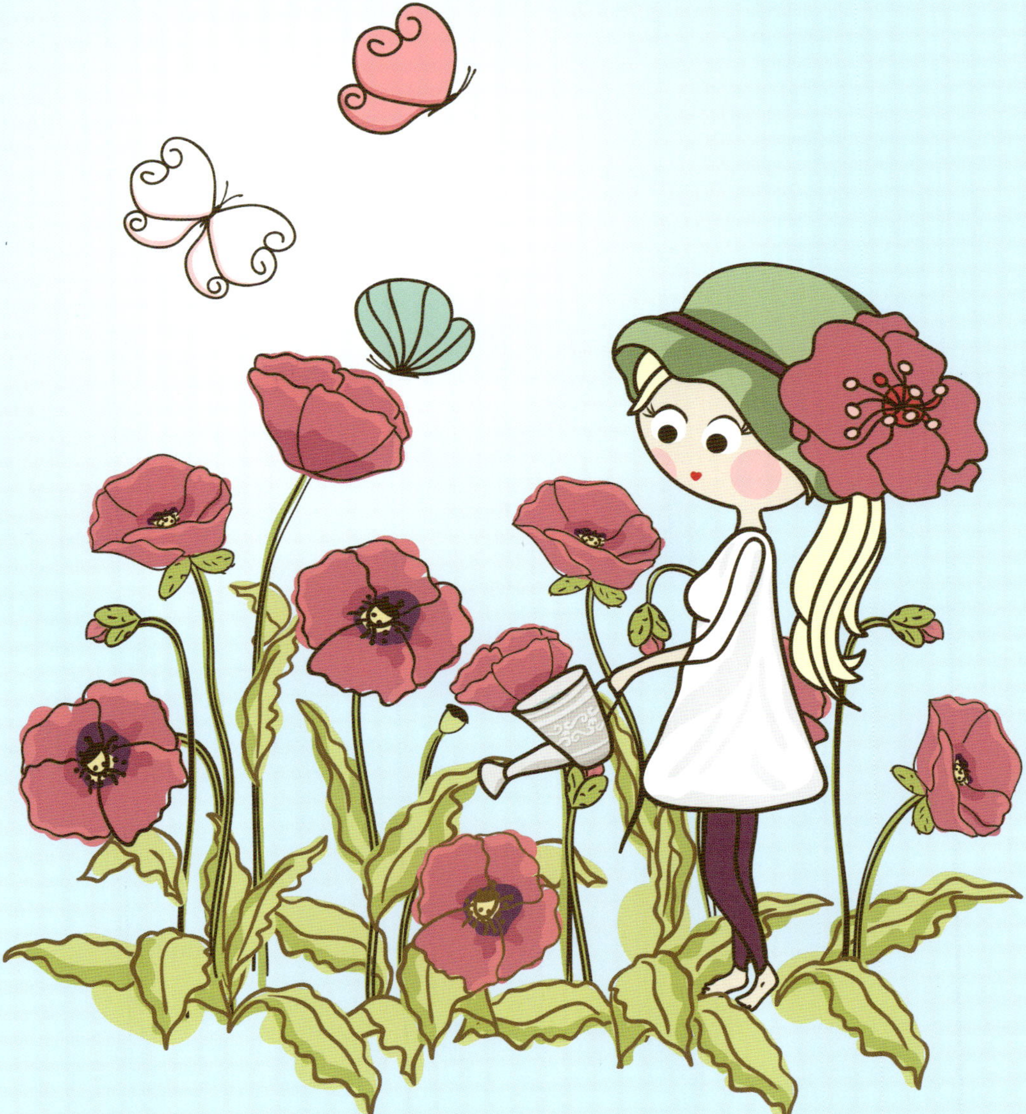

To all the children out there,
Who have lost someone dear,
Please always do remember,
That though they are not here,
You'll always have your memories,
They will forever stay,
And the love you feel inside your heart,
No-one can take away.

In spite of what you're going through,
I want you all to know,
No matter what you have to face,
God is with you and loves you so.

A Word from the author:

My Daddy died suddenly when I was 9 years old and I felt completely lost and scared without him. I knew that in The Lord's Prayer we called God "Father", so I prayed to God for His help and I asked Him into my heart to be my everlasting Heavenly Father, my Lord and Saviour. From that day in 1989, I've always called Him "Daddy God". The Lord cares so much about the tears of a hurting child and I know from personal experience that God's peace is so, so precious to a child who is grieving. I pray that you too may know the comfort of a Heavenly Father who will wipe your tears away. Simply talk to God; say and mean something like this:

Dear God,

I know that I am not always good, that I am a sinner, but I know that you love me and that your Son, Jesus Christ, died on the cross for me. Please forgive me for the wrong things that I have done in my life. Lord, I would like you to come into my life and save me. Please heal my heart from sadness. Heavenly Father please be my friend, help and guide me; change me too so I can live more like your Son, Jesus.

Amen

You can read more about the God of all comfort in the Bible:

1 Peter 5: 7
"Cast all your anxiety on Him, because He cares for you."

Psalm 46: 1
"God is our refuge and strength, an ever-present help in trouble."